Embracing First-time Students

The Retention Model That Works

Mel,

Enjoy! Give back!

I be blessed!

My Best

5/17/06

Embracing First-time Students

The Retention Model That Works

By Liz Best

Acknowledgments

This mentoring resource guide is a tribute to my daughter, Jasma. She inspired me upon her graduation, to put this mentoring concept of Project CARE into practice. I did not realize that she and a few of her classmates took advantage of the human services and resources of my colleagues who invariably mentored them.

The word **CARE** is an acronym for "Caring Adults for Residents' Existence." The Project CARE mentoring program was pioneered at Morgan State University to facilitate first−time students by an easy adjustment and transition to college life. Its success is based upon its initially targeted population of 100 first-time students which had tripled by the second semester.

I hope this book will inspire you to provide some structured human service as a Project CARE advocate to facilitate first-time students in their college adjustment for retention and academic excellence.

Table of Contents

About the Author

Elizabeth (Liz) I. Best was a Secretary at her Alma Mater in the Department of Residence Life for several years. She was uncomfortable in this role because it was very restrictive. She was convinced that if the opportunity presented itself, she would provide a more meaningful service to students.

In the meantime, she exercised her options to assume additional responsibilities as a freelance writer for several print media and as an evening instructor for Adult Education. These opportunities allowed her to meet and profile many successful business owners and human service professionals who were alumni.

Propelled by her perception and passion to be of greater service to students, she was granted permission from her immediate supervisor to birth her vision, the Project CARE mentoring program for first-time students.

After its success, she moved on and accepted a managerial position for an Entrepreneurial Development Institute. As fate would have it, however, Liz was sought-after to return to Higher Education where she was appointed as the Executive Assistant to the Chancellor of the largest Community College in the state of Maryland.

Her career of more than 15 years at three culturally diverse higher educational institutions included working as

Media Relations Director, Quality Improvement Facilitator and Adjunct Faculty.

Torn between her creativity as a part-time entrepreneur and the formality of the boardroom, she resigned to assume full-time responsibility for her own business.

Liz Best is a highly revered presenter. She has facilitated workshops as a trainer in the US, Canada, and the Caribbean. She has served as a guest on CNN and as a business consultant on radio and TV before being asked to host The Liz Best talk show online for small business owners.

Her value-added objective perspectives in higher education and for students forged her to pen this book. Read, revisit your human service to your college, new students and mentor one of them!

Preface

The title of this book, Embracing First-time Students, was selected because I wanted to convey the immediacy of warm hospitality to first-time students. This group of students is very vulnerable to many distractions during their first year at college. The word "embracing" is intended to convey personal and special attention. It is important that readers understand the emphasis placed on the personal care that first-time students will receive as a participant in this student retention model for academic excellence.

The Project CARE mentoring program was pioneered in the fall semester of 1995 at Morgan State University. The acronym, CARE (Caring Adults for Residents' Existence) is symbolic of the adult participants who served as mentors to facilitate the easy transition, adjustment and the academic success of first-time students who lived on campus.

This prototype targeted 100 first-time residents and within its first year of operation, that number had tripled. Alumni, faculty, staff and administrators from the University as well as other professionals from the immediate campus community, embraced this program for retention and academic excellence because of its unique and very humane approach.

During this pilot program, however, mentors made frequent attempts to refer several students who did not reside on campus. Those referred students had lost their academic focus and performed poorly during their first-year. More than half of them unfortunately, did not live on campus; were second-year students (sophomores) and were ineligible to participate in this mentoring program because of its emphases. Even though these students' GPAs had dropped; they were about to lose their academic scholarships or be would be expelled from school, they did not qualify for this program model.

Because of this influx of requests for Project CARE's services, the University's Retention Coordinator identified Project CARE as an excellent retention conduit for students' academic success. However, this program was exclusively designed to accommodate first-time students who lived on campus.

Statistics showed that this specially targeted population of first-year students, was identified as one that had the highest level of enthusiasm to embrace and appreciate the human service efforts of the Project CARE mentoring program.

Typically, other residents who were more seasoned and possessed advanced class rankings such as (sophomores, juniors and seniors), often displayed a stronger level of independence. Statistics also revealed that these more mature students would not be as well served by

Project CARE mentoring because of their campus familiarity and the particular program emphasis.

In addition, more-mature residents, seemed to be preoccupied with their "social" security and bonding with their classmates. While many of them might have had similar needs as first-time students for mentoring, they did not need the intense interaction, guidance, or support. They were less likely to positively respond and conform to the established Project CARE guidelines.

The practical perspectives of these two distinct student classifications – first-time and more mature students, serve as the catalyst for launching the Project CARE mentoring program and penning this Resource Guide.

This program emphasis is to make first-time residents most comfortable with their new campus lifestyles, the college environment, and to quickly adjust with alumni support, to the inevitable academic challenges that they will face. The inherent objectives of the Project CARE mentoring model help first-time residents to embrace their academic endeavors and long-term career objectives with less anxiety and/or stress.

This Project CARE mentoring program superseded other retention initiatives that existed at Morgan State University. Its intense and closely monitored human service by alumni, to first-time students has set it apart. It is very engaging and both students and alumni have options to be in the partnership for academic excellence.

Responsible/professional alumni are more compassionate about the nuances in distractions that would confront first-time students during their adjustment and transition needs. Even though the practice of senior level students has been known to mentor first-year students, it is not the same.

All students strive for the same thing-- academic excellence. It can be a challenge for a senior-level student to objectively cope with the varied issues that first-year college students have and do due diligence in as sensitive a manner. First-time students tend to respect and respond to a working adult who has achieved some professional expertise more positively.

The unique mentoring focus thrives on the generosity of committed alumni, faculty, and staff. Their designated mentoring quality time, talent, professional expertise, and resources were the essential criteria, which gave credence to the integrity and program effectiveness of this mentoring prototype.

Project CARE is a structured human service associated with accommodating first-time students at their diverse levels of need. Its format punctuates retention efforts for academic excellence with a personal touch.

Other colleges or universities whose students reside in residence halls, have retention problems, and need to get their students back on track academically, may use this mentoring model very successfully. The participants and the program philosophy are generic to any college climate whose retention rates are fledging and have student hospitality and academic success efforts as priorities.

Even though this mentoring model is designed for academic institutions, community and other organizations may find its infrastructure appropriate and flexible to accommodate their mentoring needs. The creative human service strategies shared are not bound by geographic location or organizational climate. They complement and accommodate any compassionate human service initiatives as change agents or advocates for students' academic success.

Introduction

This book is designed to encourage and provoke you to extend yourself in meeting the diverse needs of first-time students through this structured mentoring model. It includes techniques for keeping first-time students and their mentors interested and socially engaged.

As a retention tool, it provides relevant and timely strategies, options, and solutions to execute a Project CARE Mentoring program Some proven and cost-effective strategies for maintaining the program's effectiveness and integrity are also outlined.

Strategies are based upon the specifically targeted population of its prototype. They announce the program's existence, the initial student and mentor contacts, application and the recruitment strategies for participants to include, staff, administrators, and the advisory committee members (who are alumni or employees of the institution).

Operating details are provided with the understanding that a Project CARE mentoring program may be successfully instituted at any four-year college or university with residence halls.

The long and short-term goals and objectives help to cultivate and establish a "very healthy" relationship among program participants. But most importantly, between mentor and protégé.

However, it is important to emphasize that the climate of an institution, its mission and vision statements, community outreach efforts, student population, and cultural diversity should be evident components for this mentoring program's success.

The design of this mentoring program is best complemented when housed in the Department of Residence Life because of its natural communal climate.

While many of these strategies and options may be changed to accommodate the diverse program participants' level of involvement and motivation, the core components of its structure should be maintained for optimum program integrity and success.

I do not assume any responsibility for any deviation from the recommendations provided in this mentoring model. These recommendations, strategies, and options are based upon a successful mentoring program instituted at a four-year university.

The CARE Philosophy

The Project CARE mentoring program format is designed to embrace and reflect the goals and objectives of the college or university. It also complements those of the Department of Residence Life to make students as comfortable as, or more comfortable than, the homes from which they transitioned in some instances. This model lends special personal human service emphases that are as follows:

➢ To recruit "committed" alumni who will serve as positive role models to residents (students who live on campus).

➢ To help mentors cultivate committed partnerships with residents during their first year of college life.

➢ To express compassion for its residents and realistically meet them at their diverse levels of need during their adjustment and transition periods.

➢ To cultivate trust, minimize indifference, and demonstrate respect for all of its participants and the campus community at large.

> To help mentors serve as advocates for students' academic success via its socially enriching programs.

> To establish and maintain a resourceful and physically accessible group of mature professionals (primarily alumni), whose diverse training, experience, resources, and opportunities would benefit first-time students.

> To expose residents to socially diverse, culturally, racially sensitive, and enriching opportunities within the campus community.

> To create and maintain free and open lines of communication among participants and campus personnel to keep students better anchored, academically motivated and focused.

> To engage students in activities which embrace and stimulate their academic pursuits and long-term career goals and objectives.

Our Unique Perspective

Have you ever yearned for something to do that would make a positive, indelible impact and improve the quality of life for a younger person? Well, here's your chance. Through the Project CARE mentoring program you will get an opportunity to move beyond self, connect with your alma mater and honor the Golden Rule in a dynamic mentoring relationship. Remember that...

"A happy and healthy relationship with yourself radiates love, passion and energy. That energy can spread like wild fire and can touch many lives."
--Rosita Hall

While there are many types of mentoring programs, the unique perspective of Project CARE, emphasizes the need for a holistic partnership and involvement between successful alumni—on and off-campus, and first-time students. This program embraces a very sensitive and personal humane service approach to catering to the diverse needs of first-time students who live in residence halls/dorms.

This book provides guidelines and strategies to embrace, nurture, and retain new students for academic excellence. The adults targeted for this prototype were exclusively alumni, faculty, staff, and professionals from the immediate campus community.

Project CARE is a human service program of unconditional love put in action. It creates a solid partnership for academic excellence between residents and alumni. Its core strategies and guiding principles are designed to be resourceful, pertinent, and applicable to any educational institution or organization that wants to solidly support the educational endeavors of younger people who live in a campus environment.

This mentoring program model improves the retention rates, and academic performance of first-year students. Its strategies, resources, and student population are specifically designed to creatively encourage other institutions—community and faith based organizations, to embrace this program's philosophy in the most productive way. If you use them, they will work for you.

The personal interactive social sessions between mentors and residents are structured to make the college experience for first-time students most comfortable, enjoyable—fun, meaningful and positively indelible.

Goals and Objectives

Each institution's mission will dictate the culture of its residence halls and will invariably set the tone and environment for the Project CARE mentoring program. However, that culture must be able:

➢ To identify, nurture and support first-time students in an extended personal manner during their transition and adjustment period from home.

➢ To encourage and support first-time residents to improve their academic performance and increase their retention rates.

➢ To actively engage and retain first-time residents who have transferred from other institutions, live on campus, and hold a freshman status.

➢ To inform and sensitize recruited high school graduates to the autonomous demands of college life.

➢ To share with all first-time residents the benefits and significant opportunities that are inherent to program participation.

> ➢ To recruit appropriate alumni to serve as mentors and advisory committee members in the partnership for their academic excellence.

> ➢ To identify and maximize resources and opportunities that will benefit and personally embrace first-time students.

> ➢ To integrate the professional expertise and resources of mentors for first-time students' optimum growth and development.

> ➢ To establish, maintain, and improve the communications links between new students, faculty, staff, administrators, and other on-campus organizations.

> ➢ To recruit mentors who are relentlessly committed to serve as responsible role models for first-time students' academic excellence.

Practical "CARE" Strategies

Some options and strategies which keep the mentoring program participants interested and interactive are identified below. They are randomly listed because the funding, resources, support systems, and manpower, will vary from institution to institution and are only listed for functional purposes to:

➤ Identify and recruit a "manageable" group of first-time students, professional alumni, advisory committee members, and university employees who are alumni.

➤ Recruit a "two-to-one" ratio of mentors to the number of first-time students targeted.

➤ Establish communications links that will nurture social, academic growth and development for first-time students.

➤ Establish measurable timetables to meet long and short-term program goals and objectives.

➤ Establish policies and procedures for program operation and all program participants.

➤ Nurture the social, academic growth and development of first-time students.

➤ Create fun-filled social activities for optimum participation.

➤ Monitor transition and adjustment situations among first-time students.

➤ Review and assess pertinent mentoring profiles of all participants.

➤ Identify various venues to publicize the program and its benefits.

➤ Establish procedures that will complement and reinforce students' academic goals and objectives.

➤ Establish crisis-intervention and problem-resolution policies and procedures.

➤ Identify and maintain cost-containment options for operating budget and program planning.

➤ Identify other funding streams to host social events as identified by participants.

Embracing First-time Students

This program is resident-driven and does not understate its fundamental approach to meeting first-time residents' or mentors diverse needs. The Project CARE mentoring program has several unique characteristics that foster students' growth. One of them is to provide residents and mentors with the options to request a specific type of "partner" based on their diverse and personal preferences. This selection process requires several interviews and screening sessions prior to final mentoring assignment.

For mentors, some of these preferences may include age, gender, birthplace, academic acumen or major. For students it may include professional expertise, gender, age etc. Both mentors and residents are encouraged to use many of these same variables to identify partners. These options may be listed on the mentoring program application for program participation.

Caring adults who are recruited to serve as mentors must be equally as happy as students with their assignments. These assignments are important to address because they will help to maintain the level of sensitivity, allegiance to the program, a better connection to the institution and preserve the program's integrity. It is important to remember that this model is designed to embrace first-time students in a warm, friendly and caring manner and whatever it takes to ethically convey that message, the program should do.

I must reiterate that mentors should be alumni-- professionals or advocates of higher education, from the immediate campus community. They must be college graduates who express an interest in mentoring brand new college students.

When professionals from the immediate campus community are identified as mentors but are not alumni, their interviews and involvement should be, subject to a little more scrutiny because they are more difficult to "track." They are required to have a history of student advocacy or allegiance to the institution, whereby they have made some tangible donations or quantifiable service. They are also required to provide some reliable personal references. But, most importantly, their good work in higher education should precede them.

The Project CARE mentoring program has an excellent capacity to embrace, and meet many of the hidden needs of first-time students. This human service endeavor by mentors, may include varying services, gifts, or opportunities. Some of them may include sending something as simple as a greeting card to cheer up students, compliment them for getting good grades, and wish them well for birthdays or holidays. Mentors may choose to celebrate a special event or occasion by purchasing or donating schoolbooks or supplies for their protégés, or by providing personal items which would facilitate the students' preparedness for the unpredictable and diverse academic challenges that lie ahead.

The scope and substance of mentors' good deeds, duties and responsibilities may include but are not limited to intangible services. Some of them may be easily recognized during screening interviews –such as having an honest and objective listening ear. These intangible efforts should reflect the generosity of mentors' time, talent, professional expertise and resources which help to distract students' aloneness during the "high and low" periods of the semester.

Intangible expressions may also include mentors' invitations to culturally and socially enriching community activities held off campus. Some students may be invited to visit their mentors' homes during holidays and/or for special occasions (like Thanksgiving, Christmas and Easter). These expressions and invitations are important to students, particularly when students are unable to go home for the holidays and are "homesick." For the first-time student, this generosity in a non-threatening and supportive environment, nurtures and reinforces a much-welcomed atmosphere for learning and student success.

Some tangible services on the other hand, may include purchasing airline, bus or train tickets for students to go home for the holiday or if the students suddenly become ill and need to travel. Other student lifestyle services or gifts to support the adjustment and transition activities of first-time students, as deemed necessary and appropriate by the Project CARE office, are encouraged. It is important, however, to stress that tangible services, whatever they may be, are no criteria for participation in, or exclusion from the program.

Mentors need to be carefully recruited, interviewed, and selected because of the varied personal, humane services and responsibilities they will assume. Because of their written contractual commitments to serve for one year in this program, their professional expertise, and their academic experience, they are discouraged to monitor residents' matriculation beyond their freshman year. This discouragement allows the students to evolve as independent decision makers and assimilate with their fellow classmates on campus for their greater good.

While mentors may elect to keep in touch with students after the first year or two, the intense communications style and social interaction are no longer required. They my keep in touch on their own terms as responsible and caring adults.

During the students' first year in the Project CARE mentoring program, it is essential that mentors prepare them for independent decision-making skills and the academic journey only which they must futuristically walk alone. Any attempts made to sustain a mentoring relationship beyond the first year, will be solely at the discretion of the mentor because the program only requires a one-year commitment.

It is not the premise of this mentoring model to encourage or perpetuate any co-dependent relationships.

Organizational Structure

This mentoring prototype was implemented with a skeletal staff. Many student employees and other employees of the university had volunteered their services and time. However, any Project CARE mentoring program would be most efficiently implemented when the following proposed, qualified and committed staff members are hired. Based upon staff capacity and skill levels, the program administrator may identify and request more staff as needed.

This mentoring program structure is very easy to execute and "doable" for any organization with budgetary limitations. Bartering of services and resources may adequately facilitate a solid foundation for program execution without the ideal staff or specifically designated funding. Good people skills and emotional intelligence are core competencies that embody the Project CARE organizational structure.

The targeted population of 300 residents with a retention goal of 100 should accommodate the following proposed staffing structure. For this number of students, a realistic mentor-student ratio would be about three mentors to one resident. This ratio is recommended because there are more databases from which to identify alumni than there are for first-time students at any well-established university. This ratio also leaves good room for changes or mentors' availability and options to participate in the program.

Therefore, the following number of staff persons who may provide this mentoring service include:

- One full-time administrator
- One full-time administrative assistant/secretary
- Three-five student employees/aides
- Six Advisory committee members

This cost-containment of this skeletal staff, particularly as it relates to hiring college students, is based upon the student employees' work experience, skills, program commitment, and capacity to multi-task between their regular class schedules during the semester. However, a freshman with excellent organizational and people skills would work well in this setting.

The effectiveness and efficiency of this staffing combination are exclusively contingent upon commitment and passion to serve first-time students during a very critical time in their academic lives.

Mentor Identification And Participation

Mentors in the Project CARE mentoring program may be identified and selected from the alumni databases, university employee directories, fraternal, Greek, civic and other community organizations in which outstanding alumni belong or associate.

These selection resources should include and be based upon the identifiable professional expertise, maturity, caring capacity for or work with first-time students, designated quality time, accessibility and demonstrated human services to their alma mater.

Prospective mentors, however, should be poised to creatively interest and comfortably interact with first-time students as they adjust to campus life. Their objective should be to stimulate first-time students' academic interest, help them to stay focused and pursue academic excellence.

Prospective mentors should not look too young or too old to convey an unfavorable immature or overly mature impression to first-time students as their confidants or role models. Neither should their ages invite "visual biases" to minimize students' interest, respect, trust, postpone, or discourage a positive and embracing impression for mentoring. It is important to remember that younger people have their own unique perceptions and standards about appearance.

The following essential criteria qualify mentors for program participation. They include but are not limited to:

➢ Graduation from a four-year college or university where the program will be instituted.

➢ Previously demonstrated student advocacy if the mentor is not a graduate from that institution.

➢ Donation of some monetary gift or significant personal service to the institution.

➢ Campus involvement and demonstrated leadership, or human service with young adults in an academic setting.

➢ Retirees who are college graduates from other institutions, live in the community and whose positive work experience included service to new students.

➢ Stable employment in a profession similar to any of the programs of study offered by the institution.

> Retired professionals who are "young at heart" and have the capacity to intellectually interest, motivate and mentor young people.

During the mentor recruitment process, and whenever a request is made for a particular type of mentor or resident, it should be honored. Every effort to recruit capable, enthusiastic, and qualified mentors, should be seriously considered so that compatibility of the partnership for academic excellence, may be sustained. This effort enhances program effectiveness and preserves program integrity. Failure to meet any of these requests often weakens the mentoring link and distracts its best efforts to cultivate a meaningful partnership for academic excellence.

Mentors are required to make themselves available to residents once they have been assigned. They are also required to establish contact during the first week of the semester, once a week during the "drop and add" periods, and during mid and final semester examination periods. This value-added strategy for specific contacts, helps to reinforce student support and alleviate any possible anxiety a student may experience during any critical and daunting decision making times of the semester.

Because alumni are strategically, intensely targeted and interviewed for program participation, they are charged with the responsibility, and reminded periodically, to aggressively monitor the communications dynamics of their mentoring relationships. Mentors are not exempt from any of these responsibilities that may cause students tension or pressure during critical times of the semester. It is important to bear in mind that first-year students are very impressionable.

Below are some guidelines by which mentors are expected to govern themselves. They may be modified but should include:

➢ Attending the mandatory initial mentoring orientation session.

➢ Being compassionate and possess excellent, verbal, oral and sensitive communications skills.

➢ Maintaining a positive attitude to encourage, guide, and provide resources and opportunities that complement residents' adjustment to campus life and their academic interests.

➢ Setting aside at least one to two hours a week of quality time to spend with residents during the first and subsequent weeks of the semester.

➢ Being mature and proactive to facilitate new students' lifestyle needs, wants, and seamless transition and adjustment issues.

➢ Having the balanced sense of responsibility to integrate professional work ethics, personal integrity, and academic support for the first-time students' greater good.

Resident Identification And Participation

The Project CARE mentoring program does and should not discriminate on the basis of race, sex, national origin, or socio-economic status. It merely distinguishes between resident lifestyle capacities, and their cultural orientation to quickly identify and favorably respond to the first-time students' expressed needs.

The student recruitment criteria for this mentoring model are generic. They constitute and coincide with the mentoring program's unique philosophy. However, these criteria should be as diverse as the program's goals and objectives. They should also be flexible enough to embrace all students who assume a class schedule of 12 credits or more and are:

➢ First-time students who live in residence halls.

➢ First-time commuting students who express interest in the program.

➢ First-time students whose ages range between 16 and 21.

➢ First-time students with a minority status among the student population.

➢ First-time students who are first of a generation, the youngest in a family to attend college, or are "only" children.

➢ First-time students who are comfortable signing the application contract to adhere to Project CARE's program goals and objectives.

➢ First-time students who have received full academic or other scholarships or have struggled to maintain a "c" average in high school.

➢ First-time students who seem shy, withdrawn, academically challenged, high achievers, or highly-motivated.

➢ First-time students who seem indecisive, indifferent, are clearly overwhelmed, or are intimidated by the college environment.

➢ Transfer students from other colleges or universities who have the classification as "freshman," live on campus or are commuters.

It is important to note that while first-time college students who live on campus are primarily targeted to participate in the Project CARE mentoring program, transferees from two-year Community or other four-year colleges and universities are also eligible to participate in the program.

If the commuting student has established a relationship with a first-time resident, it enhances that student's recruitment status because he or she would have access to the on-campus lifestyle issues. The primary objective for targeting residents is to ensure that mentors would have easier access to communicate with their protégés and the institution can better monitor their partnership for academic excellence. The residence hall is a controlled environment.

However, transferees should be mentored delicately because of their unique status of relinquishing a once-familiar environment to attend a different school. Helping transferees to embrace the structure and philosophy of Project CARE may be a little tricky because of transferees' prior college orientation and experiences. However, it is clear to assume that their previous college experience restricts them from having similar adjustment issues as the first-time student.

It is an excellent recruitment screening strategy to raise questions about a transferee's prior college experience before making a mentoring assignment. When mentors are assigned to transferees, they should consider designating some extra time with more one-on-one mentoring sessions with them very early in the semester because students are known to have more ambivalent feelings about their adjustment than do first-time students.

While it may be safe to assume that transferees do have some legitimate and intrinsic disconnection issues with their previous schools, during their adjustment periods to their new schools, mentors are cautioned to exercise every effort to make their transition and adjustment periods very seamless. Recent alumni tend to facilitate this mentoring assignment of transferees more easily than established career alumni because of their more recent transition as college graduates.

All first-time student recruits are asked to be very responsive to their mentors' attempts to get better acquainted. Because this mentoring process and residence hall environments can be distracting to first-time students, they are gently reminded to stay focused, value the sacrifices of their mentors' time, efforts and expertise to help them. Students are also requested to schedule their mentoring times to coincide with their mentors' designated appointments to see them.

Below are some resourceful venues to identify and select first-time students for the Project CARE mentoring program. They include but are not limited to the following:

➤ Admissions, Recruitment, and Counseling Center databases.

➢ "Freshman" orientation and Honors program events and databases.

➢ The offices of International Students, Student Affairs/Activities, or Student Government databases.

➢ Personal, departmental, peer and High School Guidance Counselors' referrals.

Since the chronological ages of first-time students do not guarantee their abilities to make smooth transitions to campus life, no assumptions should be made about their capacity or reaction to embrace the Project CARE philosophy and guidelines because of its intense and interactive forums.

It is a good practice to host bi-weekly general forums for all participants and then two or more major ones during the semester. For the Spring semester, one event should be planned around Valentine's day and the other around or one week before Easter. During the fall semester, around October 31 (Halloween) and November (Thanksgiving) or just before the Christmas holidays.

Embracing this mentoring concept, for many students may need some gentle but persistent persuasion because some of them may prefer to bypass the personal sacrifices that all participants must make to nurture a meaningful partnership for academic excellence. Some students tend to be more attracted to the benefits of the program by capitalizing on mentors' expertise, their resources, and the opportunities that may give their future careers, a jump-start.

To minimize the recruitment efforts of the Project CARE personnel, high school guidance counselors may identify and prescreen students whom they believe would be excellent candidates for the program. Parents, family members, and university personnel who can confidently vouch for the program's effectiveness, are also encouraged to explore creative and viable recruitment efforts.

Because of the interest and association with the Project CARE mentoring program, mentors and student advocates invariably provide the necessary public relations service that is essential to the life and success of the program. The primary benefit of personal referrals is that mentoring may be tailored to accommodate those referred students' needs in a more intense, and personally gratifying manner.

After mentoring assignments are made, the Project CARE office follows up with a phone call to verify that either partner made some contact and a mentoring relationship was identified. In addition, the office staff contacts all participants on a weekly basis to ensure that appropriate and meaningful dialogue is going on.

First-time student participants are asked to assume the responsibility for notifying the Project CARE office if an assignment is not a good match. This level of comfort and care, punctuates the purpose for this mentoring model.

All mentors are encouraged to meet with each other mentors periodically as a group to discuss common mentoring concerns, issues, activities, and improved mentoring techniques. This gathering is generally orchestrated through and facilitated by the Project CARE office in a residence hall because of its friendly and engaging atmosphere and design. This location emphasis, simplifies the much-needed predictable access to new residents for active program participation, and impact of the stated program goals and objectives.

This mentoring program structure provides a very meaningful and rewarding experience for many professional alumni who are committed to making a difference in the lives of new students. Their human service efforts demonstrate their unconditional expressions of tangible and intangible gifts and services to benefit first-time students.

The Mentoring Mix

The mentoring mix is described as an atmosphere of "camaraderie" among program participants. However, the level of expressed interest, human service, compassion, and interactive communications exchange, give credence to the mentoring mix and keep it in its true perspective.

An orientation group meeting in the residence halls engages all program participants before they formally assume their respective duties and responsibilities. At this initial meeting, participants receive guidelines to keep the partnership fluidly engaged. This underscores the integrity of the program (See guidelines in Appendix) and cultivates greater enthusiasm and appreciation.

More importantly, first-time students are given the opportunity to observe, appreciate, and "size mentors up" before their first one-on-one meeting. Observing mentors at a distance, allows students to objectively recognize how caring, mature and eager mentors are to meet, greet and serve as their advocates for academic excellence.

This face-to-face contact in a non-threatening and very interactive social setting, is critical to this program's structure. Participants gain confidence about their roles and levels of commitment and are more comfortable setting aside "quality" mentoring time with stronger convictions. On the other hand, this meeting reduces residents' anxiety and seals the partnership for academic success more easily.

This meeting also puts the personal touch of Project CARE's human service into greater perspective. Other subsequent participant group meetings serve as essential benchmarks to monitor and control program participation, effectiveness, participants' attendance, their relationships, and levels of commitment.

Caring adults for resident's existence (CARE) are consistently encouraged to be honest, open, and accessible in their communications strategies with first-time students. This exchange in dialogue builds trust, confidence, and respect. It also identifies and demonstrates accountability and responsiveness to the program structure.

These candid conversation strategies among participants are orchestrated to seal the partnership for academic excellence between mentors and first-time students in the most meaningful and positively indelible way. Most importantly, the relationship demonstrates personal integrity and underscores their mutually signed commitments to participate in the program. This contractual arrangement commands a higher level of expectations, accountability, and responsiveness by both parties.

Occasionally the Project CARE office "jogs" the participants' memories with a phone call to maintain equal accessibility. If conflicts arise, participants are encouraged to resolve them quickly and move on with their mentoring goals and objectives. This strategy leaves no room for disrespect, disillusionment, or any brewing disappointments. It also forces mentors to be expedient in addressing pertinent issues that would rebuild their relationship if a communication link is broken. Mentors are encouraged to exercise a higher level of patience and discretion to keep uncomfortable issues in perspective.

Mentors are held more accountable for bridging all communication gaps simply because of their maturity and life experiences. Their sensitivity to students' current "freshman" status, should be the motivating factor for this mentoring mandate. It is for this reason that all participants' requests in their applications, for most compatible partners, should be honored.

To keep the interaction among participants actively engaged, periodic questionnaires should be distributed for feedback on the mentoring relationship. Identifying accurate feedback from both mentor and new resident helps to improve and sustain the program's mission and its integrity. Questionnaires soliciting feedback and program suggestions are distributed throughout the campus as well as for marketing, recruitment, and program improvement purposes.

It is important to routinely monitor program activities because it sustains participants' interests and helps to quickly identify concerns or issues, which could adversely impact the students' academic endeavors, the program's effectiveness, and its outcomes.

A critical benchmark that identifies integrity and a high level of enthusiasm for the program, is the monthly progress report that participants provide. This document provides any unusual behavior among participants-- good or bad news. It is designed so that no person's name would be disclosed and to maintain free flowing dialogue. However, the emphasis for sharing such information is placed on receiving information more than who said what. Bear in mind that no one wants to be identified as a complainer or a snitch and particularly, the first-time student. If there are critical concerns without personal disclosure, the Project CARE office, should find ways to find out what is going on and investigate the situations.

No formal written reports are required. A phone call or casual conversation is usually enough. This method of communication is important to remind participants that this mentoring model is a volunteer one. To balance this level and sense of responsibility, residents in particular, are encouraged to be less formal in sharing any information and to stop by the Project CARE office.

If mentors have concerns, they may provide similar findings in writing or by speaking with a responsible staff member if they feel the situations are justifiable.

Handling The Responsibility

Managing the responsibility of a positive mentoring relationship requires commitment, experience, insight, maturity, and sensitivity on the part of mentors (alumni) primarily. This relationship and responsibility are designed to command unconditional respect from both participants, first-time students and mentors.

Many students in the Project CARE mentoring program may exhibit blatant and irresponsible behavior because of their first real freedom to be away from home and to behave like independent adults. In such situations, mentors are poised to respond appropriately to these "growing pains" as part and parcel of the students' transition and adjustment. As mentors recognize this behavior, they should have been prepared (via mentors informal group sessions), to support these students through their trial-and-error periods of their newfound independent lifestyles.

Mentors are encouraged to be more sensitive and astute in dealing with the personal and unpredictable conduct of first-time students. However, it is safe to assume that the novelty of living away from home for the first time and being introduced to totally strange adults (mentors) may be daunting and more challenging than expected. On the other hand, this adjustment may appear as similarly restrictive as a parent-child relationship at home and cause some rebellion. In either case, mentors are cautioned to balance either of those perspectives and take better ownership of their primary roles in the Project CARE mentoring program.

As more university employees become involved in the Project CARE mentoring program, they are better equipped to address and accommodate residents' issues more sensitively. However, they are to be reminded in a non-threatening and friendly manner that students are their customers and they do provide a great percent of revenue that allows the institution to thrive as a viable business entity.

Employee participation plays a vital role to alleviate and facilitate first-time students' incidental anxiety and frustrations at many levels. The good thing is that their active participation averts any negative perceptions among first-time students. Their perceptions may include not getting answers to their questions about their specific programs of study or their general matriculation process.

In retrospect, many employees seized the opportunity to extend themselves in a more personal way and showed a better sense of concern for students in the prototype of the Project CARE mentoring program. Based upon the responsiveness in this mentoring prototype, it is easy to assume that this program format liberated many employees from their job titles and fancy offices. Without this interactive forum, it is difficult to identify what might have previously restricted this personal interaction and communication between employees and students.

The interactive forums allowed employees to behave like "real" sensitive human beings void of any perceived "attributes or accomplishments" (whatever they might have been) that governed their behavior and previously created some distance. In essence, this mentoring program structure offered no room for "egos" only for big hearts. The Project CARE mentoring model has the restorative capacity for core values, compassion, and sensitivity that sometimes lie dormant in all of us. It really does provide a win-win situation for all persons associated with an institution.

Even though all first-time students may be assigned academic advisors, getting advice and personal instructions from their mentors about their academic interests are discouraged. Unless mentors are hired in the professional capacity as academic advisors at the institution, they are cautioned to resist that temptation and defer any academic advising questions to official university personnel.

Mentors, who are recent graduates, or experts in certain professions, usually have their pulses on what course work might reinforce a level of expertise in a given program of study or profession. However, they too, are discouraged to indulge in academic advising but to share information only as a practitioner of a particular profession.

Any academic advice mentors may provide could easily be innocently misleading because many academic program requirements change without public notice for one reason or another. The bottom line for mentors is not to provide inaccurate information to first-time students because it may send them in the wrong direction and cause complications later. It is accurate to state that many programs of study might have drastically changed since many mentors were in school simply because of modern and innovative technology.

Sensitive Issues

The Project CARE program creates a very meaningful balance between human service and academics. As intellectual stimulation heightens via this mentoring model, academic interests increase. The handling of sensitive issues and the personal interaction between mentors and their protégés realistically quantify resident retention and student matriculation at more predictable rates.

Many out-of-state, only children, first generation college students, foreign or "minority" first-time students, find it easy to quickly embrace the human service efforts of the Project CARE program because of its diverse core strategies. This program facilitates successful strides beyond academic interests whereby students excel in other areas to include athletics or other student-government roles. Of critical importance is that it builds students' confidence to explore and become more comfortable with their career choices as they embrace life's many challenges.

Some exceptions to this mentoring model exist as they relate to residents and their roommates. Their roommates may be ineligible to participate in the program because of poor academic performance (low GPA's) or higher class rankings. While some of the roommates may eagerly embrace the Project CARE philosophy, their ineligibility to participate invariably impacts and influences the level of enthusiasm shared by the first-time residents with whom they may share living space.

Some specific factors which contribute to these exceptions, evolve around where and with whom the first-year student is housed in the residence hall. In some instances, first-time residents may be housed with an upperclassman, a more mature resident because of diverse reasons like: space limitation or availability, late admission or sudden roommate relocation on or off campus. These factors create territorial issues regarding space and comfort level for many first-time students.

Any social events sponsored by Project CARE in a particular residence hall that houses students with such different classifications, may only serve to heighten anxiety or frustration for the newcomer. They may also restrict the enthusiastic and innocent conversations of the first-year students about the Project CARE mentoring program with his or her mature roommate. The newcomer may become very uncomfortable to attend the social forums of Project CARE and try to escape to another place on campus for distraction and peace.

It is not a common practice to house an upperclassman with a freshman but it does and can happen. It is important to understand how some of these situations may impede a smooth adjustment period for many first-time students. Typically, mentors in the Project CARE mentoring program could diffuse these conflicts or uncomfortable situations with the help of an appropriate residence hall staff member.

This program does not ignore the realities of residents who exude fear, become frustrated or withdrawn because they may be experiencing roommate issues. The sharing of "living space" with total strangers can be an uncomfortable reality. Our goal is to make this roommate adjustment period a positive and lasting one and mentors need to understand the circumstances under which first-time students may have to live.

The protocol, sensibility and familiarity with making room assignments for a first-year student or an upperclassman, lie with the residence hall administrators. However, while this mix of sharing space with an upperclassman may help to expedite the first-time student's adjustment, and transition to campus life, it could also backfire. First-time students' adjustment periods vary. They may cause negative reactions simply because of the "fresh" face in a familiar space.

Some room assignment situations may be very intimidating and sometimes traumatic, causing abrupt room re-assignments, frustration, and a possible "staggered' start in the semester. The worst scenario from a historical perspective has been the premature withdrawal from school as the only option for many first-time residents.

By the same token, sometimes peer pressure and intimidation cause some new students to nurture low self-esteem to the point where they may become inhibited and internalize their feelings, retaliate, and exhibit negative behavior. This causes an "innocent" expulsion. I refer to this expulsion as innocent only because too many inaccurate "presumptions" are sometimes made about the adjustment periods of first-time residents (and to their detriment). Project CARE strives to provide some personal attention to first-time students' practical lifestyle and comfort levels with their roommates.

Without close communication and monitoring by mentors in this program, some common assumptions and critical mistakes can, and are often made. One such assumption is that first-time students will grow up and get over any poor roommate adjustment just as easily as the next person. However, the operant word in this mentoring program is "CARE" and so no such presumptions should be made.

However, when a designated and sensitive adult volunteers to be a mentor and extends him or herself as an advocate for the first-time student, it makes a big difference between one's perception, one's presumption, and one's reality. By the same token some better-grounded, more assertive, strong willed and better-focused first-time residents, often take flight with academic excellence. They insist on their rights to have equal access in the residence halls, maintain their academic status, and passionately pursue their academic endeavors.

Very serious attempts should be taken to monitor participating students' adjustments in the residence halls by their mentors. When housing assignments are disconnected from the constructive and creative accommodations of the Project CARE mentoring program, students suffer. The institution gets a bad reputation and first-time students are left with a negative impression.

The core principles of this mentoring model thrive on minimizing residents' poor perceptions of the institution. They are structured to improve the institution's image and foster a better sense of community for its diverse constituents. Generally, any stigma associated with first-time students' adjustments within our program, is so minute that it does not often discourage or derail the students' academic endeavors.

Mentors are reminded often that first-time students bring diverse behaviors; will have different levels of need; and will invariably respond differently to campus lifestyles. Best practices on Project CARE or the institution's part, do not always prevent the drama or trauma in room assignments.

If there is a personal violation between a mentor and a resident, such as sexual impropriety in which the victim is a student, he or she is required to immediately report this matter to the Project CARE office for assessment and immediate reassignment. Regardless of the outcome, the mentor is asked to immediately suspend any student contact so that a thorough investigation and appropriate steps may be taken to resolve and restore the student's confidence and the program's integrity.

It is recommended however, that a staff person from the Residence Life office, preferably a Resident Director, should assume direct mentoring. Professional counseling responsibilities should be given to the Counseling Center at the university so that the student may quickly heal and renew his or her confidence. Discretion and confidentiality in such situations should always be underscored as the modus operandi.

Even though Resident Directors may not be alumni, they should be counseled and primarily considered to handle these situations. This unique assignment or request is suggested because of the Resident Director's direct and immediate access to students as well as his or her managerial role for the residence hall.

The mandate for mentors is that when or if adversity arises, they are to creatively provide opportunities for residents to communicate their personal feelings, frustrations, and disappointments in a non-threatening way.

Mentors are required to create an informal support system that allows them to be favorably respond to residents' extenuating circumstances.

In spite of the different roles, mentors may assume in this program, they understand that they are not to be identified as absentee parents. Even though the temptation may be great to assume parental roles in some instances during their interaction with students, their roles are clearly defined and communicated that they should only function as supportive big brothers or sisters or as the acronym, CARE reflects-- caring adults for residents' existence.

Mentors who choose to role-play in any parental capacity, are cautioned to do so strictly based on how their mentoring relationships blossom, the communication circumstances warrant, and the mutual comfort level between them and their assigned protégés. They have to make a judgment call on how they choose to behave in their mentoring relationship.

Disclosure of any confidential information shared between mentor and student in the program is prohibited. It is important not to breach confidentiality so that open lines of communication between the Project CARE office staff, mentors, and residents may be sustained.

Important Personal Contact

In order to maintain personal contact with mentoring participants and its community-at-large, the Project CARE office distributes pertinent program information and questionnaires.   This information may be provided by letters, fact sheets, news bulletins, and postcards to ensure that the program's purpose, theme, and activities are publicized.

Some of the questionnaires include requests for feedback on program format and the social impact with participants.   The Project CARE Advisory Committee members are responsible for reviewing all of the completed and returned questionnaires to get some consensus on improving the program.

Most of this information is directly delivered to the first-time students' residence halls. Barring any unforeseen circumstances, bulk mailings to other program participants are sent at least two weeks prior to the scheduled date of a social event to their home or business addresses as mentors designate.

Forms of mail distribution may include any of the following types: "snail mail," old-fashioned and electronic bulletin boards in the residence halls, email, fliers, postcards or by making phone calls. Whichever mode is convenient and expedient to communicate any information or announcements, should be utilized.

All of the official Project CARE communications must be placed on university stationery to ensure student privacy and the program's integrity. Whenever telephone contact cannot be established with mentors or students, an official document containing the contact name, office location and phone number for a staff member should be disclosed.

Generally, a message may be distributed as a word of encouragement to students before the mid and final semester exams from the Project CARE office. Mentors may find it easy to seize this opportunity to communicate special messages to residents. Prompting phone calls are made by the Project CARE office to mentors to expedite this process because some mentors are unfamiliar with the university's academic schedule of classes or final examinations because they may work off campus.

This booster reminds first-time students of the importance to achieve academic success by staying focused or to request some special support from their mentors to minimize their anxiety or academic difficulty prior to exams.

No one should assume that mentors would remember to be this pointed and supportive because of their diverse responsibilities external to the program and the university. However, if mentors are connected to their protégées, they would know what is going on in their lives and readily come to their aid. A gentle reminder of this sort promotes personal interest and commitment in this human service endeavor. Most importantly, it validates the program's purpose and perspective on the concept of "CARE-ing."

Cultural Diversity

Mentoring first-time students from diverse cultures and socio-economic backgrounds, poses a very special challenge. It requires extreme sensitivity by mentors. Very often, culturally diverse first-time students are forced to deal with family and social issues which inhibit their smooth transition and adjustment periods.

The campus climate for many students can sometimes be daunting, turbulent, and very intense. The residual impact of those situations may also distract students from their primary objectives. It could derail their best efforts to adjust to campus life, harness their personal development, and sometimes postpone their immediate academic interests. If and when this occurs, this behavior may clearly be identified as "culture shock."

The challenge for any first-time student in the Project CARE mentoring program who experiences any cultural distractions or discomfort, should immediately solicit and identify some moral support to diffuse the situations from his or her mentor. Conscientious and caring efforts of culturally mature alumni from this mentoring program usually minimize this distress.

Mentors are cautioned to be extremely sensitive in these specially challenging situations. They are advised to be very resourceful and prepared for the unexpected. In short, mentors know that it cannot be business as usual if first-time students are going to make a smooth transition to campus life.

Being very discreet and objective are recommended as best practices for mentors to neutralize these situations before they escalate or become volatile. These strategies abort negative impressions that could defer the first-time students' academic dreams indefinitely.

A foreign, "well-traveled," or culturally competent mentor, should be assigned to mentor a "foreign" or minority student. It should not be overlooked that foreign students' immigration status and casual finances could complicate and impact the students' adjustment periods.

In many instances, some of the following cultural differences exist among "foreign" students and may include simple things like:

> ➤ The change in diet (food types)
> ➤ Eating schedules
> ➤ Adjusting to the weather
> ➤ Lifestyle and personal hygiene habits
> ➤ Comfort level with the "foreign" currency
> ➤ Adjustment to, and comfort level with new friends

> ➤ Access to appropriate clothing, school supplies or schedules
> ➤ Insufficient cash flow
> ➤ English language, colloquial expressions or mannerisms

The above-listed circumstances could be extremely stressful for any first-time student who may be many miles (another country) away from home. It is important to mention that several workshop participants during my career as a trainer for cultural diversity and sensitivity, revealed many of these discriminating and cultural adjustment realities to me.

The presumption and actions taken by a "culturally-ignorant" mentor in addressing some of these issues usually convey a strong sense of pity rather than empathy. Pity is always inappropriate even though the presumption may be innocent. Very often, many "foreign" students are insulted by presumptions—innocent as they may be, and find it difficult to articulate their feelings or be resilient to establish any meaningful relationships.

In many instances, foreign students might have invariably lived at a higher standard in their hometowns where they might have had housekeepers and other amenities that are less accessible to them in the country where they are assigned to attend school like the United States. In essence, first-time students might struggle with the adjustment of being without a lot of familiar lifestyle things. So, it is important to monitor them closely. First-time students should not be judged by the state of the economy in their hometowns; their cultural protocol or even be treated according to what the media might report. All students should be treated equally as individuals with a new lease on life and void of unwarranted prejudices.

The emotional intelligent and widely-traveled mature professionals are best candidates for mentoring these first-time students who have clearly different cultural orientations. An assignment without consideration of any of the aforementioned culturally issues, creates distance and forces the first-time student to build a "protective boundary" between the student and his or her mentor.

Here again, it is critical for many of these reasons, why some first-time students are unable to maintain their cultural pride or identity and nurture meaningful relationships with people of a different culture. All too often, this boundary or distance has been misinterpreted as arrogance.

As the "foreign" resident's self esteem is reduced, he or she becomes "culturally" uncomfortable, inhibited or insulted. It is critical to recognize that whenever there is a native language difference, a   sensitive mentoring assignment should be made.

Cultural diversity is a very delicate issue for any mentor. An astute one however, will make no presumptions about students without accurate information. It is a wise decision for an assigned mentor to take a "crash course" in foreign protocol and to do some personal research about a specific culture to embrace the first-time student. Until that takes place, chances are that no friendly or sensitive communications exchange will take place. These strategies will prevent cultural incompetence and other cultural faux pas.

The success strategy for dealing with these special challenges requires excellent communications skills and high professional standards. These skills should be inherent to the mentor's selection and qualification processes for this assignment to work well.

Project CARE mentoring program should target and strive to maintain a culturally diverse population.

Some alumni reported that being "foreign born" and experiencing prejudice was painful as undergraduate students. They were able to unequivocally detail the trauma of being culturally misunderstood. Their fear of meeting the new cultural challenges of another country made them extremely defensive and stifled some of their best efforts to rise above the value system of the United States. By the same token, some alumni were able to recall how they were able to bridge that cultural gap. Embrace university personnel and were able to cultivate life-long friendships.

The fear of meeting new cultural challenges should not outweigh the interest to nurture different ones.

Resisting Involvement

From a practical perspective, it is important to mention that all students who participate in the Project CARE mentoring program and commit to being actively involved, for some reason or other, do not always follow through on their commitment. Neither do they all respond as favorably to its interactive program structure and philosophy.

After the first week of classes, where bonding with new acquaintances develops among students (new and old friends), many first-time students tend to become withdrawn to find their independence and new identities. Other students simply assume an indifferent posture or explore other campus interests.

Some of them exude a high level of pseudo maturity and act like they are grown up. They make their best attempts to demonstrate a comfortable adjustment and transition to their new environment. Unfortunately, that pseudo maturity invariably comes back to haunt them before the end of their second semester.

Even though some students' resistance to involvement in the Project CARE mentoring program may pose some disappointment and/or immediate inconvenience for many very enthusiastic mentors, there is a solution to regain their interest in the program.

First-time students should never be forced to participate in this mentoring program—even though it is good for them. Instead, they should be encouraged to objectively look at the benefits of their active involvement and how those benefits will complement their academic goals and long-term career interests.

Exploring Budget Options

The Project CARE proposed operational budget is very cost-effective to any institution. Many of the program operations –logistics and details are executed by employees who volunteer their time and energy. They tend to have an excellent grasp on the mission and vision of the institution. They also have a vested interest in their colleagues (alumni) and the first-time students.

Most of the mentoring program activities are held on campus at the end of the business day, between 6:00 and 8:00 p.m. This time frame allows employees to transition socially right on the campus and provides the best reason for program participation. These factors significantly reduce the cost for hosting and entertaining venues.

When one sets out to implement the Project CARE mentoring program, a proposal detailing staff, their responsibilities, social interactive programs, and general administrative costs, should be carefully assessed and reviewed. This proposal should also include lifestyle issues, policies, and procedures that complement the Residence Life Department. These factors should capture the mission of the institution and the vision of the chief executive officer (president or chancellor).

Some inventory of funding sources other than those from the Residence Life Department, should be explored even though primary funding for this pilot program came exclusively from that department. Funding that supports the social activities of the mentoring program may be donated by other departments to keep participants engaged.

Bear in mind that student participants pursue diverse academic interests from every program discipline of the institution. The emphasis placed on the mentoring needs of first-time students coupled with the retention efforts of each department, should encourage every department at the institution to make a financial investment in their students. All budget options should be explored.

Funding opportunities from private citizens, businesses and alumni who do not want to be mentors, should not be ignored. Many alumni may choose to invest their personal funds where they may directly participate or readily see where their financial contributions are spent. When and if this occurs, the Advisory Committee should review the gift, record it as legitimate and appropriate, and refer it to the Budget or Development Office for disbursement and Project CARE spending.

Funding for the Project CARE mentoring program, for an example, may be explored and requested from an academic department (like Engineering). This department usually has a heavy concentration of high achievers who are culturally diverse, hail from different parts of the world and live in the residence halls with full academic scholarships. It is important to note that the retention efforts of this department were more aggressive than other departments during the life of this mentoring model.

Some other departments or schools may also have larger budget allocations and grant monies than others from the federal government to support the educational endeavors of special needs or honor students. Because of the disproportionate funding levels among departments or schools, requests to support this mentoring program population, should not be overlooked or taken for granted. I'm reminded of what the Good Book says..."ask and you shall receive!"

It is usual to have a cluster of honor students with full four-year academic scholarships housed in a particular residence hall. When this situation occurs, the Project CARE administrator should be able to quickly identify which departments may have the "deepest pockets" and serve as the "cash cows" to underwrite some parts of this mentoring program model. Their special funding opportunities, via grants, may clearly accommodate many students who are registered in specific academic programs. It would also be cost-effective to assess how this cluster of first-time students may impact program planning.

One of the more effective ways in which the Project CARE mentoring program may be able to pursue funding from different sources on campus, is to identify and formally request any unused or residual funding just before the fiscal year closes.

The program administrator must be conscientious and committed to the mentoring program's goals and objectives for this option to be efficiently executed. He or she must understand and embrace the long-term benefits, and actively advocate for the program's existence as well as its vital contribution to students' adjustment, transition, and academic success. The Project CARE administrator should be so very well connected to the institution that his or her efforts would result in some favorable funding sources if a budget is not encumbered for the program.

The primary source of information about a student's academic and retention status in this mentoring program model came from the university-wide retention committee on which the Project CARE administrator served. This committee provided quantifiable information that justified the importance and impact of this mentoring program. The more accessible such value-added information is, the more realistic requests for funding may be made to accommodate the program needs.

However, while funding may come from various streams of campus revenue, it is incumbent upon those departments, which have a larger percentage of residents who live in a specific residence halls, to understand the need and support the mentoring program endeavors. They should be sought after first as viable options for funding if other funding is not immediately identified, available or encumbered. Some schools and/or departments, which have larger budgets, tend to express more concern about their "highly-profiled" honor students' and athletes' retention rates for academic success. They often strive to provide the best comfort and accommodations to nurture their academic excellence.

If an institution is experiencing difficulty in retaining first-time students with its "tried-and-true" retention strategies, a budget encumbrance must be designated for the targeted Project CARE population.

Another important consideration for funding acquisition is through awards and grants. The Development or Alumni Offices may identify federal or private grants or other possible funding sources for the program's operating expenses. Any of these offices may identify specific funding sources and may welcome formal grant writing proposals as an alternative funding source.

If any of these options do not seem feasible for the mentoring program at your institution, engage those colleagues who might be restricted to make a direct financial contribution from their departmental budgets, and request that they reassign some contractual services to accommodate your Project CARE mentoring needs. If they are so inclined and feel they might be able to transfer funds to support staff salaries, this process may be simplified by a routine budget encumbrance.

The Project CARE mentoring program should consistently embrace all opportunities that support its efforts. The underlying rationale for these options justifies why I mentioned that the program administration must be very well connected to the program's goals and objectives as well as the institution.

When services were not bartered, creative funding sources were explored for this pilot program. Some departments, which had some residual funds from their budgets, were able to provide options for the Project CARE mentoring program. They made purchases at the University's Bookstore and Office Supply Room for some operating office supplies. Some budget line items that should be explored may include: bulk mail, phone service, office supplies, stationery, printing, postage, salaries, and refreshments.

Despite the budget options the program administrator may exercise for underwriting program expenses, a very intensive public relations campaign should be developed. This campaign will promote the already-existing program, which in turn will improve the funding options or opportunities.

A generic sample budget is omitted in this resource guide because of the diverse budgetary constraints and options at state-funded institutions. The mission and vision of diverse colleges and universities will directly reflect and impact their budgetary priorities, encumbrances, funding and spending needs, particularly as they relate to their student population and retention efforts.

The options and strategies shared in this model may or may not subscribe to any of the proposed discretionary funding options at your institution. However, these budgetary options and strategies could certainly be explored to absorb many of the proposed basic operating expenses of a Project CARE mentoring program.

These funding strategies and options, evolve around the program's prototype, which was pioneered at a state-funded institution. Private institutions may have large endowments and other funding sources that may only require a simple request.

Although it is not an openly discussed subject, and it is sometimes taken for granted, college students and residents in particular, provide one of the best streams of income for an institution. Because of this fact, aggressive efforts should be explored to encourage an institution to make special concessions to enthusiastically embrace first-time students in their adjustments to campus life for academic success.

Fortunately, the commitment and energy of alumni, faculty, and staff who participate in the Project CARE mentoring program, often provide the much-needed creative capacity and moral support which help to identify funding sources in a very focused manner.

Any funding recommendations or options exercised by the Project CARE mentoring program when no funding has been identified or encumbered, will honor the institution's commitment and customer service efforts to prepare these students for academic excellence in a very tangible way.

This program anticipates that all colleges and universities will honor and revere first-year students in the same manner as it does other revenue-generating entities on campus.

Staffing Responsibilities

<u>Program Administrator</u>

The Project CARE administrator exercises the option to discretely request support from its Advisory Committee and other university officials to maintain and improve the program's effectiveness and integrity.

He or she will assume diverse roles in this leadership capacity but primarily:

➤ Plans all program activity and identifies funding, gifts and support services.

➤ Develops and establishes program policies and procedures.

➤ Identifies and recruits mentors, residents, the advisory committee, and other support staff.

➤ Organizes and monitors mentoring assignments.

➤ Supervises and monitors the mentoring relationship.

➢ Creates mentor and resident student directories and databases.

➢ Convenes and attends pertinent miscellaneous on and off-campus related meetings that may impact first-time students' adjustment and retention.

➢ Serves as liaison between mentors and residents, residents and the campus as identified.

➢ Delegates work assignments and responsibilities to staff.

➢ Composes and edits miscellaneous correspondence, reports, newsletter, and other pertinent official correspondence.

➢ Prepares and supervises public relations campaigns, efforts and activities.

➢ Establishes and monitors timetables to meet long and short-term program goals and objectives.

➢ Designs and implements crisis-intervention and problem resolution policies and procedures.

➢ Manages cost-containment budget expenditures.

➤ Develops strategic plans to bridge communications gaps between mentors, first-time students and employees.

Advisory Committee/Honorary Mentors

Members of this group represent faculty, staff, retirees, campus administrators, and one first-time student resident. This mix of people facilitates an objective perspective for decision-making and effective program planning.

In some cases, alumni from other institutions may serve on this committee. However, they must have been faithful supporters of the institution and possess excellent leadership skills, which complement the goals and objectives of Project CARE mentoring.

The Advisory Committee meets monthly to monitor and arbitrate controversial and troublesome resident lifestyle issues throughout the semester. They facilitate program development decisions, interview and screen mentors who are not alumni of the institution. When the majority of these members are employed on campus, telephone conference calls are made in lieu of scheduled meetings. This helps to expedite decisions regarding mentoring issues such as residents' crises, emergencies or conflict .

Honorary Mentors of the Advisory Committee may include those persons who do not want to commit to the mentoring responsibility but want to support the efforts of the program. In their respective roles, they:

➤ Serve as resource persons to gauge the transition and adjustment periods of first-time residents.

➤ Interview and screen prospective mentors who are not alumni and student recruits who have extenuating circumstances.

➤ Review the operating budget, other funding streams, and proposals and sometimes underwrite some program activities.

➤ Assess and review controversial and sensitive mentoring situations.

➤ Recommend solutions to sustain and improve program quality.

➤ Review and summarize completed questionnaires and periodic mentoring reports.

All committee member assignments are voluntary. Members serve in this capacity for one year so that they may become familiar with the other participants of the program. However, they are required to notify the Project CARE office at least two weeks prior to the next scheduled meeting if they decide to terminate their services early.

Advisory committee members provide an invaluable service to oversee the design of communication instruments used in the program. They are also responsible for providing objective perspectives about the mentoring program.

Administrative Assistant/Secretary

➤ Manages office operations and follows through on administrative details.

➤ Attends and convenes meetings in the absence of, and on behalf of the program administrator as needed.

➤ Supervises all office support staff and serves as Time Keeper.

➤ Takes minutes at meetings and maintains records of all program activity.

➤ Researches mentors' and students' profiles and data bases.

➤ Distributes public relations announcements on and off-campus.

Clerical staff

All persons who work in this capacity are identified as students on work-study or campus employment as a cost-containment effort. Therefore, the scope and level of their responsibilities are contingent upon their class schedules, free time, and skill levels. In their respective roles, they may:

> ➤ Perform a variety of clerical and customer-service work, data entry, and retrieval.

> ➤ Type, answer the phone, and follow up on mentoring contacts or assignments by phone.

> ➤ Photo copy miscellaneous correspondence, send faxes, and tabulate a variety of data.

> ➤ Serve as hosts and hostesses at mentoring events, deliver and distribute bulk mail.

> ➤ Periodically run work-related errands across campus.

> ➤ Post signage and miscellaneous announcements on campus bulletin boards.

A Psychological Perspective
by
Henrietta Hestick, Ph.D.

For many years, considerable attention has been focused on mentoring children and early adolescents. In contrast, mentoring advocates have ignored older adolescents and youth who attend colleges and universities as a group of interest. Child and adolescent mentoring programs were developed and promulgated with little attention to college residents, racial/ethnic, cultural, gender, and other demographic differences.

The Project CARE mentoring program has drawn attention to the unique experiences of this group. Despite some of the college programs which are in place and which give increased attention to these undergraduates, awareness of, and sensitivity to mental health needs and psychological well-being, they are unevenly dealt with.

For the most part, colleges and universities continue to develop and utilize programs for new residents without making appropriate adjustments based on their unique needs and diverse experiences.

College and university officials are reminded in this resource guide of the unique experiences and needs of first-year residents. When adolescents and youth leave home to live on campus, they are faced with such issues as emancipation from family, adjustment to new living situations as well as the overriding goal to stay in college, do well academically and graduate. The pressures of examinations, tests and term papers required to be successful, are compounded by their anxieties of basic daily living, particularly in a new environment.

The results of the National depression Screening day recognized at many colleges and universities have indicated that surprisingly high numbers of students showed symptoms of depression and were referred for psychological and/or psychiatric treatment. Project CARE provides an early interventionist program where Caring Adults for Residents' Existence seek to bridge the gap between home and campus; between feelings of loss and experiencing a sense of connection; and between support and falling through the academic cracks.

I commend the innovators of the Project CARE mentoring program and thank them for working towards the retention of residents and the reduction in the number of students who are "at risk" for academic failure and social-emotional difficulties.

———

Dr. Hestick is a college professor and a licensed clinical Psychologist.

Evaluation and Assessment

An end-of-semester internal evaluation instrument is essential to ensure program quality and integrity. The Advisory Committee of the Project CARE mentoring program and its administrator should provide information to facilitate this process. However, most of the information used to evaluate and assess this program, should be retrieved from the completed questionnaires which program participants would have completed throughout the semester.

The external evaluation instrument should include and be structured to accommodate, the diverse activities of the program. It should also include the adjustments, transition, and retention efforts of first-time students and their mentors.

A good strategy for preparing this type of evaluation instrument would be to request that one of the behavioral science departments at your institution (like the Psychology or Sociology) design or prepare it. Either of these two departments should be familiar with the technical evaluation format.

Once the department prepares the evaluation instrument, it should provide information that would quantify and assess the program's integrity, its effectiveness, and recommend ways to improve the program.

To ensure objective improvement strategies for the services rendered to all first-time students, each of the below-listed departments that deal directly with new students or provided some program funding should be given a copy of this evaluation report by the end of the semester to include:

- The Alumni office
- Advisory Committee
- The Department of Residence Life
- The Retention office
- The Office of Student Affairs
- The Counseling Center
- The International Affairs office
- The Student Government office
- The Student Activities office
- The Office of Admissions and Recruitment
- The President/Chancellor's office
- The Grants and Budget offices
- The Development office
- The Office of Records and Registration

Meeting first-time students at their diverse levels of need, particularly during their adjustment and transition periods, may only achieve maximum success when there are caring and committed adults who are enthusiastic about making a positive difference in the lives of new students.

Conclusion

Prioritizing the diverse needs of first-time students who live on campus is the reason for this program. As you reflect on the Project CARE philosophy, strategies, and options provided for starting and executing this mentoring program, you will notice how much emphases were placed on making first-time students feel special.

When responsible adults achieve a certain level of professional success, they generally want to share their expertise in a tangible and unpretentious personal way if given the opportunity. In this mentoring model, alumni are given the opportunities to be as generous as they want to be in assisting first-time students in their adjustment to their diverse campus lifestyles. Mentors are expected to maintain a formidable presence in the lives of first-time students via the one-on-one and interactive group forums held in the residence halls.

More importantly, these alumni will get a chance to value the social interaction with their peers. Many of them will reflect on their undergraduate years and recognize that they did not have, or were exposed to such a well-orchestrated support system as the Project CARE mentoring program. Even though they may openly acknowledge the support they received during their undergraduate years, they will recognize that they did not receive the same level of personal attention or intense support to reinforce their academic endeavors or career goals.

The strategies and options in this book are practical and can be used by any mentors in similar student setting. They will alleviate or deter negative cross-cultural communications. Mentors will share their undergraduate frustrations, good and bad experiences to benefit, embrace and enhance the lives of first-time students.

The level of CARE that this mentoring model provides should not be ignored because the good, bad or ugly things we all do, invariably come back to haunt us when we least expect. So, it is important to give a little bit of yourself — the best of yourself to benefit others. The old adage, *"an ounce of prevention is worth a pound of cure,"* does directly correspond to the positive things mentors will share with students. Beside that, mentoring is personally rewarding!

The quality control of the communications strategies in this program, do reiterate to the first-time that an institution truly cares about his or her adjustment, retention and academic success.

Even though some of the strategies and options may seem repetitive, they are by design. Repetition reinforces learning and it begins with graduates (alumni) who model positive behavior for new students. This intense support during a student's first year of college, underscores a student's confidence and improves the student's academic performance. It prevents the first-time student from being easily distracted by the diverse "everyday" campus lifestyle issues and improves the retention rates.

One cannot ignore the relief many out-of-town parents get when they know that there is a responsible former graduate supporting and advocating for their children's retention and academic success. With escalating tuition, many parents are concerned about their financial investments in their children. This program alleviates their anxiety. Parents understand the pain and disappointment of unexpected student expulsion or involuntary withdrawal for one reason or another.

Many of them have expressed great appreciation for this prototype. Parents do understand and recognize how their children's good intentions and academic interests can be distracted and derail their lifestyles. Some of them are fully aware that there is no tuition refund if their children do not adjust well to campus life and have to drop out of school. This human service will help to educate them on the value-added benefits of the Project CARE mentoring program.

By the same token, mentors fill those gaps that may require surrogate parental support to keep students better focused. In essence, the Project CARE mentoring program maximizes the expertise of alumni in a very caring and holistic way to benefit new students.

It gives an institution a positive and solid public identity, better credibility for caring for its students and a competitive advantage to receive government funding when there is a higher retention and academic achievement rate. When student retention rates are high, the student academic performance rates increase; the institution gains a positive reputation and is positioned to attract the best of students.

Institutions are better positioned to be more selective in their recruitment efforts and raise their academic standards. Project CARE protects and uniquely cares for first-time students with diverse situations. Its goal is to achieve optimum student adjustment, retention, and academic excellence.

Those students who might be in awe or are intimidated by the magnitude of the college experience, will have their fears alleviated by the support of mentors and assimilate better among peers and the campus community with great ease.

For your quick personal assessment and appreciation for the Project CARE mentoring model, here are the four beneficiaries of this program:

1. First-time students who live on campus.

2. Parents of those students.
3. Alumni who serve as mentors.
4. The institution (and its community at large).

This program provides a "win-win" situation for all of the constituents of an institution.

APPENDIX

Parent Information Letter

July 15,

Dear Ms (Parent or Guardian):

The Department of Residence Life is pleased to announce a human service initiative to support your son's (or daughter's) transition and adjustment to campus life. It is the Project CARE mentoring program and it is designed exclusively for first-time students who live on campus.

The word "CARE" is an acronym for Caring Adults for Residents' Existence. These adults will primarily be alumni, faculty, and other university personnel who will serve as mentors. They will provide meaningful and supportive opportunities for your child during his or her first year on campus.

Our objective is to help your child to stay better focused on his or her academic interest. Our "hand-picked" mentors are professional people. In rare instances alumni from our immediate community and who are associated with this university, will also serve as mentors.

Please find enclosed the Project CARE brochure for your review and general information. If you have any questions or concerns, please do not hesitate to call me at _____.

I hope you have a wonderful summer and we look forward to working with your son (or daughter) real soon.

Sincerely,

Resident Acceptance Notice

August 30,

Dear Cindy (New Resident):

I am happy to respond to your expressed interest in the Project CARE mentoring program at the Freshman Orientation session held two weeks ago.

Please complete the enclosed application and be sure to select your preference for a mentor. Because we want you to find the most compatible mentor, you will need to indicate your preference on the application. Please also review the enclosed accompanying Resident Guidelines to participate in the program.

Our office cannot make an assignment until we have received your completed application. If you have questions, please do not hesitate to call me at (   ) _____between 9 a.m. and 5 p.m. any Monday through Friday.

I look forward to seeing you at our first social scheduled for _____(detail, date, time and place). Your personal invitation will be sent to you as soon as we receive your application.

I look forward to seeing you soon and enjoy the rest of your summer!

Sincerely,

Resident Application

Project CARE--Caring Adults for Residents' Existence
  Office Address: _____
  Phone: (   )_____

_____*Classification*____/_____
  Name   *New   Transfer*

_____ ____ ____ _____
  Home Address   *City* *State*   *SS#*

_____ _____
  Campus Address   *Phone #*

_____ __ __ __ _____
  Parent's name   (M   S   D)   *Phone #*

_____ ____ ____ _____
  Siblings   *Yes   No*   *Name(s)*

_____ _____
  Major   *Career Goal*

Would you prefer a ____male____ or female mentor?

*Will you support your mentor's commitment to get
adjusted to campus life?_____yes_____no.*

*If you have a crisis, do you promise to inform your mentor
____, Project CARE___or____ Residence Life staff member?*

*My signature below implies that I do agree to do my part in
 establishing a mentoring relationship through Project CARE.*

_____*Signature* _____*Date*

Resident Guidelines

1. *Attend the mandatory Project CARE orientation meeting.*

2. *Keep an open mind and be respectful.*

3. *Show appreciation for mentor's time, commitment, and expertise.*

4. *Model mentor's positive attributes for career objective.*

5. *Establish trust, respect, and confidence in your mentor.*

6. *Share information about your adjustment and academic interest.*

7. *Keep scheduled appointments and call if you are unable to do so.*

8. *Provide contact information for mentor.*

9. *Inform the Project CARE office of any changes in your contact information or mentor relationship.*

10. *Attend all Project CARE's social functions.*

Resident Assignment Notice

August or September (Date is contingent upon room confirmation)

Dear Cindy (Resident):

I am enclosing your mentor assignment information and contact information for your mentor as follows:

Mentor's
Name_____Address_____
Phone_____work_____home

Should you have any questions, please call the Project CARE office at _____. It would be in your best interest to read the Mentor's guidelines so that you would know what to expect of him or her. It is similar to the one you previously received only that he or she has some specific responsibilities that will help you adjust better to college life.

Please try to meet your mentor in person at our first social gathering. Be sure to give him or her your contact information, your name and phone number so that you could be reached. Remember that your mentor's time as a professional, is very important and he or she has other professional commitments.

Please let us know if this assignment is a good match for you. Thank you and see you soon!

Sincerely,

Resident Follow-up Questionnaire

November 1 (Fall semester) or March 1 (Spring semester)

Dear Cindy (address him or her by name):

I hope that your relationship with your mentor is working out as expected. Please complete the enclosed questionnaire and return it to our main office so that you may pick up your free Project CARE souvenir (T-shirt).

Your name_____campus address_____
Assigned Mentor_____Phone_____

1.Have you seen or heard from your mentor?___yes___no
2.Is the relationship working?___yes___no.
3.Would you like to be reassigned? ___yes___no___not now___
4.Are you going away for the Holiday break?___yes___no.
5.Are you enjoying campus life?___yes___no.
6.Please give us two of your friends' names and phone numbers
   you would recommend to join our program below.
        Name_____Phone_____
        Name_____Phone_____

7.State briefly any concerns or difficulties you have with the
   program:_____

Thank you and please call us at_____if you have questions.

Mentor Information Letter

August 15,

*Dear Mr., Ms. or Dr.*_____

Thank you for consenting to serve as a mentor with the Project CARE mentoring program. I am delighted that you have identified and taken time out of your busy schedule to mentor a first-time student.

Please review our enclosed brochure, Mentor Application and Mentor Guidelines so that you may review, complete and return to us. Making this decision to help a first-time student in his or her adjustment and transition to campus for academic excellence is a significant human service.

Our office cannot make an assignment until we receive your completed and signed application. Please be sure to indicate your preference in mentor, whether you would prefer female or male. Please call us if you have any questions at:_____during the week between 9 a.m. and 5 p.m.

On behalf of the Project CARE mentoring program and all of its participants, we welcome you and thank you for your interest in making a positive and indelible impression to cultivate a partnership for academic excellence. I look forward to seeing you soon.

Very truly yours,

Mentor Application

_____Alumni Status____/____/_____
Mentor Name   Employee/Retiree/Affiliation

_____ ___ _____ _____
Home Address   City   State   SS#

_____   Phone
Business Address   S M D W_____
_____ _____   _____
Other contact name   Phone   Marital Status: Circle one

_____ ____ ____ _____
Children living at home Yes   No   How many

_____
Academic Major   Career Goal/Job Title
Would you prefer a ____male____ or female first-year student?

Do you promise to provide best mentoring practices that support your protégé's endeavors in his or her transition to campus life?____yes____no.

If you have to postpone or cancel an appointment, do you promise to inform your protégé or call the Project CARE or Residence Life office early?____yes____will try____

If resident has a campus crisis, could you accommodate or provide lodging for one to two nights? ____yes____no.

My signature implies that I will promote a wholesome mentoring relationship with a first-time student assigned by the Project CARE office. _____
                    Signature   Date

Mentor Guidelines

1. Mentors should have obvious self-esteem in tact.

2. Be comfortable talking about their positive role models and if they don't or didn't have one, they should be relentless and committed to being the best role model.

3. Attend the mandatory Project CARE orientation meeting.

4. Be warm, friendly and professional at all times.

5. Cultivate meaningful partnerships for residents' growth.

6. Teach residents to set long and short-term goals.

7. Be conscientious and supportive to residents.

8. Downplay their weaknesses.

9. Keep dialogue fluid to assist resident with campus adjustments.

10. Be positive, attentive, and objective and observe residents' body language.

11. Reinforce good impressions, establish and nurture trust, and respect.

12. *Encourage the expression of dreams and the importance of keeping an open mind.*

13. *Be flexible but maintain firmness.*

14. *Inform the Program administrator of changes in contact information.*

15. *Nurture sound values and de-emphasize material ones.*

16. *Expect the best in residents and acquiesce to mediocrity.*

17. *Provide progress reports on the relationship for academic excellence.*

18. *Return completed questionnaires from Project CARE.*

19. *Teach residents self-reliance; nurture sound decision-making skills.*

20. *Be resourceful; handle residents' identified needs discretely.*

Mentor Acceptance Letter

August 30,

Dear Mr., Ms., or Dr._____

Congratulations! You have been selected to join the ranks of some outstanding alumni who have consented to serve as mentors. We have received all of your information and will do all that we can to find you a suitable match for this partnership for academic excellence.

Please note that during the first week of September, we will have our first orientation/social gathering for all participants at 6 p.m. It will be held in the Multipurpose room of ____residence hall. Please be sure to return attendance confirmation when you receive your formal invitation. Light refreshments will be served.

There will also be a mandatory mentors' meeting on Thursday, September 18, at 6:30 p.m. in the Multipurpose room of _____residence hall where you will get to personally meet all mentors. This meeting should be about an hour and half. So please come prepared to meet, have fun and fellowship.

We welcome you and any suggestions you may have to make this event a memorable one. We are very happy to have you become an active part of our first-year student retention efforts. Should you have any questions, feel free to give me a call at ( ) _____.

Sincerely,

Mentor's Prayer

Dear God, teach me to be a good mentor.
Help my protégées to look forward to meeting me.
Let them trust my judgment.
Let me provide them with resources to deal with uncertainties.
And allow me to understand my protégées.

Father, please give me an objective ear to listen patiently.
Give me tolerance for their anxieties and personal concerns.
Help me to be courteous, kind-hearted, and understanding.
Forbid me from laughing at their suggestions.

Let me not offend them by my demeanor.
Allow my words to be the true reflection of my heart.
Keep me from intimidation or dishonesty.
And let your light shine through me.

Dear God, let me teach them self-reliance and discretion.
Give me wisdom, understanding, and compassion.
Let me be politely self-assured, humble, and approachable.
Allow me to be a good confidant during troublesome times.
Help me to influence them to become very responsible adults.
And father, please let them succeed in all that is good.

Amen

Mentor Assignment Letter

August or September

Dear Mentor

I am enclosing your protégé assignment and his or her contact information as follows:

First-time student name_____
Residence   Hall_____
Phone_____Personal/Cell_____

Please call our office at _____if this assignment is a good one for you. Your protégé also has some similar guidelines as you did with similar types of expectations for your partnership for academic excellence. He or she knows that you have a very hectic schedule and has identified some quality time to mentor him or her.

We invite you to meet your protégé in person at our first social gather. Be sure to give him or her your contact information where you might be reached and the times that would be most convenient for you.

If this assignment is not a good one for you after your first couple of meetings, please let us know. We thank you for your time and interest in the program and look forward to a wonderful semester!

Sincerely,

Mentor Telephone Follow-up

October 1,

Good morning Mr., Ms., or
*Dr.*_____*(use mentor's last*
name). My name is _____*and I am*
calling on behalf of Project CARE to follow up on your contact
with _____*(name of the resident), your assigned*
protégée. (Wait for acknowledgment or response).

I hope your relationship with _____ *(call the student's) is*
working out as you anticipated... In case you can't remember
his or her name, it is _____*. His or her campus*
address and phone number are _____*(residence*
*hall)*_____*(phone).*

1. *Have you seen or heard from your protégée?*
   yes___no___.
2. *Is the relationship working for you?___yes___no.*
3. *Would you like us to reassign you another resident?*
   _____yes___no___not now____next semester__.
4. *Would you like to have an additional resident assigned*
   to you?___yes___no.
5. *Are you going away during the holiday?___yes___no.*

Please note that on _____*(day and date)*
*at*_____ *(time), all Project CARE participants will meet for*
a social gathering on campus. There will be some refreshments
so please look out for your invitation in the mail for more
details. Please plan to join us.

If you have any questions, please call our Program Director,
_____*Mr., Ms., or Dr.*_____*at*
_____*(phone number) or stop by our office at*
_____*(building name and room number). Thank you for your time and interest in Project CARE. We really appreciate your commitment.*

*Caller's name*_____
*Date*_____

Recommendations

The strategies complement programs that have a common place to congregate and execute interactive social programs. Private high schools that have dormitories or residence halls may easily incorporate many of these strategies.

Other organizations and institutions that do not have residence halls, such as faith-based and community organizations, would find it more beneficial to get some personal consulting on their mentoring interests.

However, before embarking on any mission to execute a Project CARE mentoring program, it is important to honestly answer the following four questions:

1. Do I have an immediate pool of young people with common characteristics or goals?

2. Where and how would I find committed and responsible adults to serve as mentors?

3. Do I have an appropriate and reliable place or location for mentor/protege interactions or social exchange?

4. What are some of the cost-effective and cost-containment options I may comfortably exercise to get started?

Printed in the United States
67760LVS00002B/403-498

9 781601 450210